To all my fans
but above all to those
who are willing to admit
that they don't already know
all the answers!

Sexuality &

Sexual Techniques

ISBN 978-0956894-724

Published by *Nosper Books* 2015

Copyright © Jane Thomas 2015

Revised & updated 2021

www.nosper.com

Contents

I   Sex information must explain real women's behaviours

The young tend to be the most sexually active. So mature couples with decades of experience often assume that young people know more about sex than they do. In turn each generation rejects the wisdom of its elders. The sex researchers' findings have been so contentious that their work is simply ignored. So today we have no universally accepted account of our sexuality and sex information is based largely on personal intuition.

The fundamental principles of scientific method include observing the real world, proposing theories to explain our observations and testing those theories to see if they are correct. This does not happen in sexology. Unpopular research findings are ignored rather than investigated and adjusted as necessary. While sensational proposals are promoted on the basis of popular appeal. These theories are not tested to ensure that they can be accepted into an accumulated and consistent body of scientific knowledge.

I use logical thinking, basic common sense and a knowledge of the prerequisites for orgasm (based on my own experience of masturbation and on what men need to orgasm by any means) to propose a theory about how orgasm is achieved. I suggest it is unreasonable to expect women to replicate the unrealistic sexual feats claimed by a tiny minority. What is impossible for me to achieve is probably equally impossible for other women.

I have been capable of orgasm all of my adult life. I have also been adventurous with a lover but nothing worked until middle age. Even then the climaxes I have had with a lover are very pleasurable physical sensations but I do not place the same emotional significance on genital stimulation that men do. It is simply not possible for other women to respond so totally differently. If they did, there would be significant numbers of women in the general population able to provide explicit accounts of how they achieve orgasm as a response to erotic stimuli. This is clearly not the case. Very few women are willing to say anything at all about sex and orgasm.

It has taken me years of analysing my most personal sexual experiences (both alone and with a lover) for me to be able to describe not only what happens in my mind and to my body but also to suggest perhaps why.[1] In presenting this evidence, my challenge is that no one can accept that sex information today is so wrong! We'd rather base our sexual knowledge on a concoction of fantasy and ignorance than the research findings. So it's small wonder that both sexes end up feeling inadequate and (even worse!) blaming a lover for not making sex as exciting as we think it should be! The embarrassment over sex is due to our unwillingness to accept the facts.

1

II   Understanding men's sexual and emotional needs

Male masturbation frequencies[2] vary significantly, indicating not only a range in responsiveness, but also the different conscious choices men make over how they enjoy their arousal cycle from erection to ejaculation.

Sex is emotional for men because it connects them with lovers, family and society. Male mammals are often solitary creatures. They interact with other males in order to defend territory and with females in order to mate. Men tend not to share their thoughts and feelings as readily as women do. So we say that women are emotional and men are not. Yet men often use aggression (an emotional behaviour) to express anger, frustration and fear.

When facing an enemy it is helpful if we can avoid being paralysed with fear or bursting into tears. We need to be able to channel any anger and apprehension we may feel into aggressive action. So aggression is considered a strength because it is an asset if we are facing a physical threat. Tears, on the other hand, are thought to be a sign of weakness. The accompanying emotional state can be debilitating. There is nothing wrong with having a good cry as long as you are not trying to fight off an enemy (which women are not designed to do). Crying is one way of venting our emotions.

A man tends to make a better aggressor and defender because his testosterone levels help him respond more effectively in high pressure situations. Testosterone impels men to take risks (some more than others obviously!). Overall men go for much higher stakes than women are willing to play for. Despite our modern and sophisticated weaponry, films still depict actors in arm-to-arm combat or wrestling. A hands-on fist fight expresses the emotions of a more personal form of combat. Men fight (and play sport) to help dissipate the tensions generated by their sex and personal drives.

Men can certainly be distracted by a beautiful woman. But it is only a distraction. They are much more concerned about the threat of another man. Men may insist that sex is vital to their welfare but their territorial instincts come first. Some put work before a relationship while others rate the comradeship and adrenaline rush of a sporting event over a sexual opportunity. Despite men's sex drive, it is usually women who make relationships work.

Males fight each other for breeding rights and they lose the opportunity to mate if they cannot beat rivals. Females mate with males who win rights over resources (to sustain a family) and who can protect them from other males. In human terms we observe that women tend to gravitate towards men who can provide protection and lifestyle through earnings or status.

2.1 Male adolescence: differentiating orgasm from ejaculation

For sexually precocious boys, half have an orgasm by the age of 7 and two-thirds by the age of 12. But until they start ejaculating, such orgasms are one-offs or sporadic. Most boys (90%) ejaculate for the first time between the ages of 11 and 15. The average white male has his first orgasm that leads to ejaculation by the age of 13 years 10½ months (13.88 years).

Ejaculation (of semen) and male orgasm are two separate phenomena. It is possible for a young boy to orgasm without ejaculating. But once a boy reaches adolescence (assumed to coincide very approximately with his first ejaculation) he most normally ejaculates every time he has an orgasm.

Some men believe that ejaculation is possible without a preceding orgasm but they are confusing orgasm with the concept of orgasmic pleasure.

Ejaculation does not involve mind-blowing pleasure every single time because the sensations that accompany orgasm inevitably vary. We feel varying degrees of sexual pleasure depending on the physical and psychological (erotic or emotional) circumstances that give rise to orgasm. There is no physiological event other than orgasm that could trigger ejaculation.[3]

Some male prostitutes climax five, six or more times per day regularly over many years. Even with such high frequencies, although the quantity of ejaculate is lower than usual, a little semen is always produced. Around three quarters of men do not ejaculate with any force. Their semen is merely exuded from the glans. Other men may ejaculate semen over distances of a few inches or even a few feet (rarely up to more than a meter!).

Biological changes to our bodies that are beyond our conscious control attract our curiosity. Women can be fascinated with the changes in their bodies during pregnancy just as boys can be fascinated with their penis during puberty (and beyond!). At puberty girls get breasts and periods: body changes linked to their child-bearing role. Few girls focus on masturbation as boys do. The male arousal cycle explains the difference. Boys are fascinated with their responses but girls experience nothing equivalent.

A man takes pride in his ability to achieve an erection. He enjoys not only the sensations of his physical and mental arousal but also the pleasure of being physically stimulated (even by himself) when erect. The visual evidence of his erection adds to a man's sexual arousal. Consequently men (unlike women) like to observe their genitals as they stimulate themselves to orgasm. A man is aroused by what he sees and by objects associated with sexual activity. His own erection is simply one of those associations.

2.1.1 The male arousal cycle from erection to ejaculation

Sensations of fear, apprehension, shock or surprise all give rise to nervous system responses that have characteristics in common with arousal. Some young boys initially orgasm[4] in response to many of these kinds of stimuli. But over time adolescent boys come to associate their arousal with psychological stimuli (erotic turn-ons) that are explicitly sexual. They also become increasingly reliant on specific penile stimulation for orgasm.

The sources of first ejaculation are masturbation (two-thirds), nocturnal emissions (in an eight of the cases), intercourse (one boy in eight) and homosexual contacts (one boy in twenty). Wet dreams are most common (71% of men) between 21 and 25 when the highest average frequency is about once in three weeks (0.3 per week). By the age of 50 only a third of men have sex dreams, which do not average more than four or five a year.

For a fifth of men (22%) orgasm is primarily a genital reaction while nearly half of men (45%) have some build-up (body tension). The remaining four variations are similar to the first two but can include additional trembling, fainting, frenzied movements, convulsions, collapse, laughter and talking.

As for other male mammals, men are aroused by smells and secretions. A man takes a pride in his erection and ejaculation. A man may want to ejaculate over a lover's body or to enjoy a woman urinating over his testicles as she rides him, stimulating his penis with her vagina. Men enjoy sharing details of anatomy, secretions and responses. Men want to display themselves specifically when they are aroused and have an erection. Women do not seek out similar stimuli nor are they aroused by displaying themselves.

Although men enjoy being touched just about anywhere, they foremost hope that a lover will stimulate their penis (by hand, by mouth and ultimately by offering penetrative sex). Looking at and interacting with their own genitals, as well as those of a lover, is emotionally significant to men. Intercourse completes a man's arousal cycle thereby providing his sense of emotional well-being. So ejaculating into a vagina has a special emotional significance (not for gay men!). But there is no parallel for women.

A man's interest in his own penis comes from his frequent or regular state of arousal. His interest in the genitals of the opposite sex comes from his sex drive to penetrate a female. A woman conversely is neither spontaneously aroused not does she actively seek penetrative sex. This explains a woman's sexual passivity with a lover. She has little interest either in obtaining stimulation of her own genitals or in stimulating a lover's genitalia.

4

2.1.2 The symbiotic relationship between men and women

When living in an environment devoid of sexual stimuli (such as one without women) most men cease all forms of sexual activity. For example, the arousal cycle of men, who are locked up in prison with no access to any kind of visual media (magazines, television and internet), grinds to a halt.[5] This illustrates an interesting relationship between arousal and sex drive. A man's sex drive may be triggered by his physical proximity to a lover.

Men's responsiveness decreases with age because male orgasm depends on the physical process of maintaining an erection. Masturbation is the first major outlet to disappear from men's sexual histories, which indicates that male arousal stems foremost from sexual activity with a lover. Men who leave their wives for younger lovers feel younger (and more virile!) because of the ease with which they are aroused by a young woman's body.

Imagine growing up alone on a desert island without any contact with other people. As a female I am confident that I would have no reason to discover orgasm. My only source of arousal is the awareness that men are turned on by my body. My fantasies focus on male responses, male sex drive and the idea of penetration. In other words, without men I have nothing to fantasise about. Of course the same is true for a boy growing up on a desert island. Very few boys (0.81%) experience spontaneous ejaculation. Both masturbation and sex dreams depend on a person's use of creative imagination either by remembering or embellishing an experience with a real-life lover.

My own sexual awareness stemmed from when men first noticed my breasts. The function of the female breast is clear: to suckle a babe. But breasts also represent the anatomy that most clearly distinguishes women from men. Women's bodies are sensual because they are soft and fleshy (while men's are firm and muscular). Although they are just as responsive at any age, women are less attractive to men when they no longer look fertile. This explains why young women are more motivated by casual sex. It's not just that men find young women attractive but that an older woman feels less desirable because of the reduced interest she receives from men.

We talk about love as a selfless emotion but often there are more selfish needs involved. Children love their mother because of the nurturing care and protection she offers. A woman loves a man who is willing to defend and support her. Her willingness to offer him intercourse, ensures her own survival. A man loves a woman who is willing to offer him regular intercourse. By protecting her, a man is also safeguarding his prime sexual outlet. We tend to love those people who provide for our emotional needs.

2.1.3 We all carry the potential to be homosexual in our genes

Women typically get on well with homosexual men. Gay men often have the social skills that women appreciate but straight men tend to lack. Homophobia is largely down a certain kind of heterosexual man, who disrespects men (and women) for being on the receiving end of penetrative sex. Modern films often make references to the (grossly exaggerated) occurrence of prison rape, thereby perpetuating unjustified prejudice. Men who vilify gays may be repressing their own predilection for homosexuality.[6]

The law tends to focus on anal intercourse rather than homosexuality (lesbians apparently threaten no one). In Britain, the Buggery Act of 1533 legislated for consenting adults to be punished (by death until 1861) for what they did in private and reflects the massive taboo surrounding anal sex.

Alan Turing (famous for breaking The Enigma code and saving thousands of Allied lives during World War II) was one of the victims of this legislation, which made homosexuality a crime. Offered the choice between prison and hormone treatment (equivalent to castration) he chose suicide. It was only after The Sexual Offenses Act (1967) that consenting adult men (over the age of twenty-one) could legally have anal sex in private. For a time in the UK we then had the incongruous situation where anal intercourse was explicitly legalised for gay men but not for heterosexuals.

In 1994 The Criminal Justice and Public Order Act established equality once more by setting the age of consent at 18 for all homo- and heterosexual activity (later lowered to 16 by the Sexual Offenses Act 2003). Anal intercourse was thereby legalised (implicitly) for heterosexuals to legislate for sexual equality rather than as a response to demand from heterosexuals.

While 50% of men are straight only 4% of men are exclusively gay. Some men are aroused by both sexes and a surprising number (37%) have at least one gay encounter that ends in their own orgasm. Many of these are one-offs or sporadic. Some men resist homosexual urges because of the taboo. Yet homosexuality is evidently an aspect of humanity shared by all of us.

Some gays (notably lesbians) do reproduce. But relatively few children are fathered by gay men compared to those fathered by straight men. Yet research indicates that the relative number of homosexuals in the population remains steady over time. Responsiveness to homosexual stimuli surfaces in random individuals. There is no biological justification for homosexual behaviour but given humans are highly successful reproductively, perhaps like left and right handedness, homosexuality is just a harmless variation.

2.2 Age is the foremost factor affecting male responsiveness

Factors that affect men's orgasm frequencies include their age, the age at which they reached adolescence as well as their level of education.

Age is far and away the most significant factor in male sexual performance. [7] Men are most sexually active in late adolescence. Thereafter their responsiveness declines very gradually. A significant upside to this aging process is that older men are able to spend longer enjoying sexual activity.

As men age, the frequency of their early morning erections decreases. Also the time over which they can maintain an erection reduces (from an average of over one hour in late teens to 7 minutes for 66 to 70-year-olds). The angle of elevation of the erect penis varies considerably between individuals but also reduces as a man ages. The average position for all ages is slightly above the horizontal. Around 15-20% carry the penis at 45^0 above the horizontal while 8-10% of men have an erection tight against the body.

Some men, particularly the less educated, refer to women, who may be sexually available, as chick (US), bird (UK) or sheila (Australia). Men covet an attractive woman as if she is sexual property (or sex object). So why do young women accept older lovers? Why do they not want a young man who is not only more attractive but also more responsive? Women are attracted more by the lifestyle a man provides than by his sexual talents.

Men often assume that women with years of experience will be less enthusiastic about sex. Men gravitate towards younger women not just because of their attractiveness but because they are more amenable. Naivety and inexperience cause young women to be more easily impressed and exploited. Men's sex drive and their arousal gives them a natural authority in obtaining the erotic stimuli and physical stimulation they need from lovemaking. So there is no advantage to a woman being sexually experienced.

Men assume that a woman is always aroused and willing to engage in intercourse. Yet men will only engage in sexual activity either when they have an erection or when they are confident of being able to achieve one. Young men can be like a wound-up spring and persistently hassling a partner for sex. It is easier for an older man to accommodate a woman's sporadic sexual interest. I have found the quality and variety of sex play has increased over the years but the frequency has remained at a similar level.

Male impotence is relatively rare until old age. At 70 years of age only 27% of white men are impotent but by 80 this has increased to 3 out of 4. The continuing amenability of a man's partner is doubtless also a factor.

2.2.1 Boys who are adolescent first have the highest sex drive

For practical purposes male adolescence is assumed to coincide with a boy's first ejaculation. Boys who become adolescent first (before 12 years of age) often have the highest orgasm frequencies throughout their lives.[8]

Statistics can be misleading. For example, men are taller than women on average but some women are taller than many men. Similarly a group defined by certain characteristics may have a higher responsiveness on average than another group defined by different characteristics but someone in the second group may be more responsive than many in the first group.

Masturbation frequencies are highest among men who become adolescent first. Around 99% of such men masturbate compared with 93% of men who reach adolescence later than the average (13 years old). Highly-sexed men are also slightly more likely to engage in homosexual activities.

Having a creative imagination affects male responsiveness. Boys with a high IQ (intelligence quota) are often those who reach adolescence first.

There is a link between masturbation frequencies and creative imagination. Boys only start to use fantasies once they have some sexual experience (either alone or with a partner). A boy engages in fantasies (at least to start with) because he enjoys remembering a real-life episode. He uses his memories (perhaps enhanced over time by imagination) to achieve what initially occurred spontaneously or through physical stimulation alone.

Few boys masturbate before the onset of adolescence. Only 10% of boys are masturbating by the age of nine and only 13% by ten years of age.

Men's responsiveness is a defining characteristic of their sexuality. Males are drawn to other male bodies (even animals) because they are fascinated by the very evident male responses. A man's arousal is not only visible to the naked eye it is also easily perceived by a lover because of his shortness of breath, his weakness at the knees and his involuntary moans of pleasure.

I accept that I am biased but I have to agree with gay men. Sexually, men are much more interesting than women are! Perhaps this explains why male fantasies tend to focus on exaggerating women's true responsiveness.

Men's sexuality revolves around a focus on the penis. Men are fascinated with how the penis responds (male arousal cycle) when stimulated. Men's sexual behaviours include a desire to display their erect genitals. A man wants an appreciative lover to admire his responsiveness. But many women may feel uneasy providing sex talk that involves putting on an act.

2.2.2 Masturbation and fantasy require a creative imagination

Masturbation is least common among less educated males (89%). More men who are high school educated (95%) and who are college educated (96%) are involved in masturbation for at least some period of their lives.

There are two suggestions for why college boys masturbate more than less-educated boys. The first is that college girls are not as easy to get into bed so college boys have to resort to masturbation[9] more than others. The second is that being educated is associated with having a good imagination, which is needed to achieve the arousal implicit in masturbating to orgasm.

Only 92% of men masturbate. In other words out of every hundred men 8 never masturbate. Some boys have their first ejaculation through intercourse. They may never masturbate because they have intercourse sufficiently frequently that they never need the additional sexual outlet. Other men have a sufficiently low sex drive that they have no need to masturbate.

Some boys are more promiscuous than others. They may seek out girls who are more sexually willing or they may be less discerning about sexual opportunities. It seems likely that the less intellectual have more frivolous sexual encounters than those who are more considered about their choices. Some men choose to limit their opportunities to the more ideal scenarios.

Masturbation frequencies after marriage are highest (69%) among men who are college educated. Only 42% of men who are high school educated, masturbate after marriage and only 29% of the least educated males. Married men masturbate when intercourse is unavailable. But equally some men choose to masturbate because they enjoy the variety of sexual outlet.

Men differ in their sexual behaviours within marriage according to their educational level. Less educated men start by combining married life with infidelities but become more faithful over time. More educated men start marriage by being faithful but end up having extra-marital affairs later on. Sometimes this male infidelity is actively encouraged by the wives as long as they know that they have the financial security that marriage provides.

Although Kinsey found that a forceful personality is not an absolute guarantee that a man will have a high sex drive, he did conclude that there was a tendency for men with what he called a high metabolic rate, including many boys who reach puberty first, to be among the more highly-sexed. Religious men have average orgasm frequencies up to at least a third lower than comparable males who are not devout. It is possible that those who have a lower responsiveness are more willing to adhere to religious codes.

2.2.3 Heterosexual relationships involve mismatched sex drives

Men are naturally responsive. So no man should feel inadequate about ejaculating quickly.[10] Men accept the misconception that women might be able to orgasm through intercourse if stimulated long enough because they want to prolong their own enjoyment of intercourse. Any sense of inadequacy over male speeds to orgasm could be easily overcome if a man was willing to stimulate a woman (orally or manually) regardless of his own state of arousal. Nature ensures that men's sex drive focuses them on intercourse, which is designed to facilitate male orgasm (and ejaculation).

Men stress about what they can do or say to impress a woman enough to get her into bed. So they are frustrated when a date does not result in sex. Most women need time to develop an emotional connection before intercourse feels appropriate. But an experienced woman knows that any relationship with a man involves an on-going commitment of continuing to offer regular sex. So although it's only one time, it's usually the first time out of many. A man more or less assumes that the arrangement is on-going.

A very wise man said *"I try to keep my wife happy because I know that if she is happy she will keep me happy!"* But if sex is so vital to men, why are they forever getting it wrong? Heterosexual relationships involve a woman subjugating herself to a man in sexual terms and a man subjugating himself to a woman in emotional terms. So men sometimes prefer work to home where they feel disadvantaged by women's emotional dominance.

You would think men who love women would always protect them. Yet it is straight men (not gay men) with their predilection for aggressive behaviour who disrespect others for being physically weaker. Heterosexual men may love women and they may be willing to support them but they only do this for women who offer them the regular sexual interaction men need. Women may even accept being beaten as natural if they love aggressive men. For most of human existence a woman's survival has relied on having a man to protect her (mostly from other men). In return she was obliged to offer intercourse even though women commonly died during childbirth.

A man's dilemma is his dependence on a woman to provide the significant pleasure of intercourse. A woman's dilemma is her complete indifference to intercourse, which she is obliged to provide regularly over decades. Rape is not related to male sex drive. Men who rape do so in order to dominate, control and humiliate others. Rape Crisis UK reports that *"around 85% of survivors/victims know their attacker prior to the rape or assault and that often this violence is perpetrated by a partner or ex-partner."*

2.3 The conscious and subconscious components of sexuality

Human sexuality has biological, emotional and intellectual components.

The biological aspects are innate (we are born that way) and beyond our conscious control. Males of all species have a direct instinct to mate that females do not have. Women need to be persuaded to accept intercourse.

For both sexes there is a huge range in responsiveness (frequency with which we orgasm) that defines normal but on average men are up to 6 times more responsive than women. Also the need to be sexually active (to the point of orgasm) plus the need for regular opportunities to engage in penetrative sex with a lover are much more emotionally significant to men.

The emotional aspects of our sexuality are determined by our personality. Some people are less inhibited about engaging in genital activity outside a relationship. Others are looking for emotional reassurance to varying degrees. Women who are sexually provocative or who are emotionally needy (attention-seeking) may be perceived to be sexual to the extent that they facilitate sexual activity even if they themselves never have an orgasm.

Regardless of gender, some people prefer to have sex with someone they love. Others are motivated more by lust. Men's sex drive focuses them on obtaining their own pleasure. Whereas women are more likely to need an emotional context to enjoy lovemaking fully. Some women may interpret their own emotional neediness (their desire to be valued) as sexual desire.

The intellectual aspects of our sexuality depend on our imagination. Some people define sex purely in terms of interaction with a lover. They may consider any kind of solitary activity or activity that is not directly required for reproduction to be a perversion. Others find pleasure in these non-reproductive aspects of their sexuality. They enjoy fantasy, erotic turn-ons and stimulating themselves to orgasm quite separately from a relationship.

Most people view sex as a basic biological or emotional experience. Relatively few people positively seek out abstract eroticism. This explains why so few people are interested in discussing sexual pleasuring: not just what they might enjoy themselves but also what they are willing to offer a lover.

There is a difference between a platonic kiss (given to a relative or friend) and a sexual kiss with a potential lover. A sexual kiss conveys a man's urgent drive to have intercourse and he looks for a woman to communicate her willingness to cooperate. In a sexual relationship, intercourse defines the minimum sexual activity that a woman is expected to be amenable to.[11]

2.3.1 Some men hope that sexual pleasuring can be mutual

Society often implies that sex (like smoking and drinking) is a sign of maturity and worldliness. Films portray prostitutes as beautiful and classy young women offering a variety of sexual pleasuring techniques. Sadly, the run-of-the-mill prostitute does not provide 'dinner with a show'.[12] She feels no obligation to fake her presumed pleasure in return for charging her client. Around 69% of men admit to having had sex at least once with a prostitute but only 20% ever use prostitutes regularly. Younger (under thirty) and less educated men are most likely to have sex with prostitutes.

It would be logical to assume that any sexual activity a man pays for is likely to revolve around male gratification. But some men want to feel that sexual pleasuring can be just as important to a woman as it is to them. An educated man invests in sexual pleasuring (beyond intercourse) to reassure himself that he is not being selfish. Such men are less tempted by casual sex because of the lack of emotional context. Their ability to enjoy fantasies may substitute for the variety that other men obtain from promiscuity.

Some men are more emotionally sensitive than others. A more intellectual man is often timid in approaching women. He respects women's mysterious sexuality. He is aware of how easily his mother, sisters and girlfriends are offended by sexual references. He hopes for intimacy but wants to obtain a woman's approval before he is confident to make a sexual advance.

A man's willingness to stimulate a woman (even if only through intercourse) reassures him that his motivations (because they are aimed at pleasuring his lover rather than himself) are unselfish. Men's sexual needs are biological; women's are emotional. A woman offers sex for money, for love or for vanity (ego). Men assume women have sex to enjoy orgasm even though Kinsey and Hite highlighted that women orgasm most easily by masturbating alone rather than with a lover. Today the only statistics quoted from their work are Kinsey's 10% of women who never orgasm by any means and Hite's 30% of women who orgasm through intercourse.

No one explains why they quote these statistics while ignoring others. The findings from this early research were so unpopular that no one has obtained funding for research to confirm or correct the findings. Therefore we have no other reliable statistics. Modern surveys never justify how they select their samples, their tiny sample sizes or the appropriateness of extending their findings to every woman worldwide. Our society has rejected the conclusions of women in the population because of the conflict with the much more attractive way that women are portrayed in erotic fiction.

2.3.2 Many men prefer intercourse and never offer any foreplay

The men with the highest overall orgasm frequencies throughout their lives are the less educated (those who are not educated beyond high school).

Some men focus on enjoying their own responsiveness rather than a lover's arousal. Their self-absorption makes them relatively oblivious to a lover's perspective, who is relieved of any need to exaggerate her arousal. This behaviour is slightly more typical of those who are less educated. They lack the emotional sensitivity of the college boys. These men assume (or don't care about) female arousal and just focus on their own orgasm[13]!

Some men (perhaps the majority) are interested foremost in a woman's physical appearance and her sexual willingness. They may enjoy casual sex for the opportunity to experience first-hand the variation in the genital anatomy and physical responses of a new partner. They may appreciate exploring new techniques and approaches to sex play. Men respond most readily to sexual activity with a lover. So it makes sense that less educated men (who masturbate less but have intercourse more) have more orgasms.

Sex manuals suggest that a man should offer foreplay before heading for his own orgasm through intercourse. But as Kinsey noted decades ago, foreplay appears to make very little difference to women's arousal levels.

Some women assume (because of porn or erotic fiction) that everyone's sex life routinely includes foreplay. In fact, marital sex focuses on intercourse, which is all most men need to obtain their sexual release. A more sensitive man may feel obliged to invest in a lover's pleasure. He may have read about the need to reciprocate and, consequently, want to reassure himself that sex is not a selfish male pleasure. A woman accepts whatever stimulation a man offers within the limits of what she is comfortable with.

Men tell me that none of their lovers has ever had a problem with orgasm. But if you ask them what pleasuring or erotic turn-ons their partners enjoy they have no answer. A man in his sixties said *"unless the women I have known persistently, consistently and convincingly lied about what they were experiencing then I don't believe the problem is as wide-spread as you clearly do"*. He refused to discuss the subject further. Yet this man had a string of ex-wives each of whom had taken a share of his assets. A woman lets a man believe his fantasy of arousing her through intercourse because intercourse involves minimal effort for her. Naturally women are also silent on this topic, thereby creating an implicit lovers' pact with sexual ego on one side and a desire for a supportive relationship on the other.

2.3.3 Men may get more sex if they are willing to be realistic

Only some men like to offer their partners any form of foreplay. Other men (probably the majority) prefer to head straight for the joys of intercourse.[14]

Because men are much more promiscuous than women on average, it is often assumed that all men are promiscuous. Many men think about having sex with various women throughout their average day. But this does not mean that all of them would take up the opportunity even if they were offered it! Some men are much more tempted by the thrills and pleasures of promiscuity than others. Other men look for an emotional connection.

Kinsey told of couples who lived in rural areas, who had sex three times a day (around meal-times) every day for years. It is clear that this sexual activity would be quick. Specifically, it would not involve extended foreplay, focused on assisting with presumed female arousal. But this modern obligation, that men have acquired in the light of women's demands for equal rights and a less subjugated sexual role, has created unrealistic expectations for the time and energy couples want to invest in sexual activity.

The average time a man lasts (from penetration until ejaculation) is about two minutes, which is hardly onerous. But when a man wants to spend time on foreplay prior to intercourse, sex becomes harder work for the woman. It is not just the time involved but also the need to appear engaged! Ironically the man, who simply takes, is likely to have more sex because he expects little performance from the woman. A woman can enjoy being the object of a man's desire without needing to falsify her responsiveness.

Female orgasm is promoted as if it is a relationship accessory. But orgasm is a highly specific genital response that arises because we ourselves (not our partners) want it. In the first place, only we can determine what explicit aspect of sexual activity is particularly arousing to us personally. Secondly only we can generate the mental focus required for orgasm. This psychological arousal is then combined with massaging the blood flow within the erectile organ (penis or clitoris) to achieve a release of sexual energy.

Very occasionally (as a more mature woman) I ask my partner to stimulate me to a climax (through clitoral stimulation most usually combined with anal intercourse). I do this if I feel some glimmer of arousal because I know that it is so important to him to be able to pleasure me in this way. It seems odd to me that something, which is supposedly for my pleasure, is in fact for his. The climax I enjoy is much more vital to my lover than it is to me.

14

III   Understanding women's sexual and emotional needs

Sadly, researchers are often just as impressed with far-fetched accounts of female orgasm as the general public. Academics debate pure conjecture such as female ejaculation (copious quantities of vaginal juices produced by aroused females) based on age-old male fantasies and up-suck of sperm (pelvic contractions supposedly arising from so-called vaginal orgasms) as if they are proven facts. Most women ignore these myths fabricated by men but a few enjoy publicising this appealing account of their sexuality.

Orgasm can be used as a defining aspect of men's sexuality because of the ease with which male orgasm can be objectively identified and justified in terms of men's sexual behaviours. The same is not true for female orgasm. One problem is the assumption that women experience orgasm in exactly the same circumstances that men do. Another is that female responsiveness is defined in terms of women's willingness to offer a man an opportunity for intercourse rather than their motivation to achieve their own orgasm.

Kinsey's research indicated that women orgasm once in 2 weeks on average versus men's 3 orgasms a week (men under age 30). Men slow down with age but even by 60, male orgasm frequencies have not fallen to female levels. In fact, Kinsey and Hite overestimated female responsiveness. Their conclusions were incorrect, not because their sampling methods were flawed, but because they accepted what women said. They did not validate these orgasm claims. For example, the anatomy involved in orgasm has to be consistent for all women (regardless of sexual orientation) whether they are alone or with a lover (regardless of their lover's gender).

It is difficult to find a definition of sexual politics because the term encapsulates the unpalatable fact that men exploit women but men are also manipulated by women who take advantage of men's sexual needs. Men obsess about female orgasm because it is elusive in reality. Pornography exaggerates female responsiveness to provide turn-ons that assist with male orgasm. After all, if porn reflected reality, it would no longer be a fantasy! A fantasy, by definition, is an enhancement or an exaggeration of reality.

Men's politics is characterised by violent action and women's by manipulative silence. But silence proves nothing. I know we all want a man to think us the sexiest thing in the world but it is not helpful to have female sexuality defined in such a way that most women refuse to comment! The evidence for female responsiveness needs to come from women who can talk confidently about their enjoyment of arousal (a response to erotic stimuli) and orgasm resulting from sexual activity they themselves initiate.[15]

3.1 Female sexuality is defined by men and their fantasies

Men's acute arousal ensures that they approach sex with a clear agenda. Women are not aroused, which is why they talk about emotional sensations.[16] Whether in real life or in pornography a woman provides an orifice (mouth, vagina or anus) for a man to ejaculate into. Women rarely demonstrate sexual initiative. For example, they do not commonly suck a man's nipples, his testicles or stimulate his anus orally, with fingers or a dildo.

I am challenging modern beliefs about female sexuality, which I believe are wrong. For example: if women masturbate during sex, why are so few men aware that the clitoris is the source of female orgasm? And if women orgasm easily through oral sex, why do men complain that women seldom return the favour by offering fellatio? But also why would anyone ever ask about female orgasm with a lover? Intercourse involves stimulation of the vagina while female masturbation focuses on the clitoris. If every woman masturbates, why do so few comment on the difference between the two?

Research findings from polling women in the population (such as those of Kinsey and Hite) were so controversial that the approach was abandoned. Research that involved observing couples having intercourse under laboratory conditions (such as that of Masters and Johnson) was more popular. Researchers simply explained the orgasms these women were assumed to have and then extended their conclusions to the rest of the female population. No one ever questioned the assumption that women must orgasm at some point during male thrusting but before a man is obliged to ejaculate.

Today researchers use ultrasound machines to measure minute changes in blood flow in the pelvic region. They assume that these physiological changes equate to what men call arousal. But what use is female arousal if women are never consciously aware of experiencing any erotic pleasure? They also place electrodes in women's vaginas and assume that electrical impulses equate to what men call orgasm. But what kind of orgasm is it when so many women are unsure about whether they have ever had one? No one sticks anything into a man to figure out what turns him on and what stimulation causes his orgasm. Blood flow may increase in the genitals for various reasons. It may indicate that a woman is subconsciously preparing for sexual activity, such as intercourse, that has nothing to do with orgasm.

How do female researchers expect to discover something from the public that they themselves do not know? When you orgasm, not only do you know for sure but you also know how you got there! This is because orgasm arises from resolving erotic (psychological) stimuli in our own mind.

3.1.1 Men's sexual knowledge is acquired from pornography

Today we have no official account of human sexuality. So men's sexual knowledge of how women enjoy sexual pleasure (how women are assumed to achieve orgasm) comes from pornography or other fictional sources intended to cause arousal. For example, so-called squirting is completely fictional. Women cannot ejaculate. Similarly, the female breast is no more capable of producing an orgasm than the male breast would be.[17]

Some people are wise enough to appreciate that pornography is a fictional world that revolves around providing male turn-ons (fantasies) that assist with male orgasm. But pornography is often blamed for men's sexual ignorance. There is nothing new about men fantasising about unrealistic feats they hope attractive young women are capable of! These turn-ons have existed in the heads of men of every generation since time immemorial. It is the widespread promotion and ease of access that is fairly recent.

Men never witness a woman masturbating to orgasm. So a woman meets male expectations for female orgasm by emulating porn actresses. We are so used to women keeping men happy or pretending to do what we assume they should be capable of. The idea that women can enjoy their own responsiveness is less intuitive. This aspect of female sexuality focuses on what women do for themselves quite independently of men. It has little to do with sexual activity based on intercourse culminating in male orgasm.

Men's bravado involves exaggerating the number or variety of their sexual opportunities and lovers. Women's bravado involves boasting about orgasm. But their modesty and their inability to be explicit clearly indicate that they are referring to emotional sensations rather than erotic responses. Who ever heard of a man who continues to stimulate a partner and engage in sexual activity once he has had his orgasm? Male orgasm defines the end of heterosexual activity because men initiate and drive sexual activity with a lover. We confuse arousal with true orgasm. So pornography depicts women being aroused and constantly re-aroused. Fictional orgasms are portrayed as a state of endless euphoria. This is of course total nonsense!

Orgasm is just one part of the sexual arousal cycle, which varies but is a unique experience. The ideal scenario involves enjoying psychological stimulation (conscious erotic fantasy or subconscious response to eroticism) combined with genital stimulation (of the aroused sex organ: penis or clitoris) that culminates in the release of sexual tension (in the form of an orgasm) followed by a pleasurable aftermath (of orgasm) including waves of post-climax echoes and sensations of relaxation and lassitude.

3.1.2 Female sexuality involves attracting male sexual attention

Any discussion of female sexuality is usually aimed at providing turn-ons for men rather than being a realistic description of how women truly orgasm. Those who are paid to promote sex succeed in confusing us all (even women) over what is truly possible. Women who talk about orgasm are either promoting their therapy business, their personal services or their sexual ego. Sadly we are easily duped by the supposed exploits of others!

Some women mislead men into believing that they are satisfied either to end sex sooner or to satisfy a man's need to feel that he has not been selfish. What strikes me as odd is that the only evidence men seek of female responsiveness is that women should be enthusiastic about intercourse. Surely if someone was truly responsive you would expect them to talk of their enjoyment of turn-ons? Surely, they would masturbate occasionally?

Men's sex drive means they naturally seek out women who are amenable to intercourse.[18] A woman accepts that a man's sexual admiration is based on the hope that she will be amenable to offering him regular intercourse.

Some women get an ego boost from exhibiting their sexuality. In an attempt to be more convincing, they try to justify their orgasms (which was what the fictional G-spot has been used for). But isn't it a wild coincidence that women, who boast about orgasm, are basically telling men exactly what they want to hear? Not only is female orgasm possible with a lover but it occurs within the two-minute timeframe offered by intercourse!

Only a handful of women describe experiences that reflect popular beliefs about female sexuality. Most women never comment. Until millions of women support these stories, they remain in the realm of erotic fiction! Women's inability to reconcile their amazing good luck with the experiences of millions of other women make it clear that they are seeking political goals rather than enjoying their own responses. Those who are truly responsive (men for example!) don't promote their own orgasm. They discuss their enjoyment of erotic turn-ons such as their lover's orgasm.

There are countless sources providing a porn-friendly, over-hyped view of female sexuality (that portray women as if they respond sexually just as men do - to the same physical stimulation, to the same psychological turn-ons, within the same timeframes and with the same frequency as men do). My work is for liberated and worldly couples who understand that male and female sexuality are fundamentally very different. Sadly few people are capable of being honest with themselves let alone with a sexual partner.

3.1.3 Bisexuality indicates an ambivalence over a lover's gender

Although men have varying levels of sex drive (which affect the frequency with which they want sex), once a man engages in specific genital stimulation he almost always does orgasm.[19] For men, physical stimulation leads to orgasm because they are easily aroused, especially with a lover.

A man's sexual emotions involve his sexual drive to engage in penetrative sex and to enjoy the eroticism of being physically intimate with a lover. A woman's sexual emotions involve demonstrating her love by responding to a man's desire for intercourse in return for her lover's appreciation, gratitude and affectionate response. We see a parallel in this difference between the sexes in the gay world where homosexual men are often highly promiscuous with casual sexual encounters proceeding quickly to genital action. Lesbian women, on the other hand, tend to have longer-lasting, sometimes platonic relationships, involving strong emotional attachments.

Only 2% of the female population is exclusively homosexual (half as common as male homosexuality). Lesbians do not always use genital techniques but those who do are more effective at achieving female orgasm than is usual among heterosexuals (whose lovemaking rarely includes techniques aimed at facilitating female orgasm). Lesbians are likely to be older before using stimulation techniques aimed at causing orgasm because young women's minds and bodies do not respond easily with a lover. Many women (regardless of orientation) prefer other pleasures over sex.

Women who fantasise may be able to deduce their orientation from the nature of their fantasies. Alternatively we could define a heterosexual woman by her desire to attract male sexual attention. In women, bisexuality may indicate an ambivalence to a lover's gender. Lesbian and bisexual women don't talk about what turns them on or what they enjoy about sexual activity with a lover any more than other women do. They talk about their concerns for gaining political and social acceptance of their sexuality. Lesbianism may simply indicate a preference for female companionship.

Women adopt the role of dominatrix as a male turn-on. But playing such a role is unlikely to provide a female turn-on nor does it assist with female orgasm. The biological female role is submissive to the dominant male. Men may want to adopt a submissive role with a woman because they fantasise about the woman taking the initiative and stimulating the man for a change. They may also like to imagine that her initiative indicates that she is sexually aroused but female arousal is much more obscure than this. Sexual activity of any kind is likely to involve some variant on domination.

3.2 Understanding what works: the clitoris versus the vagina

Regardless of gender, sexual activity that is aimed at achieving orgasm involves continuous rhythmic movements[20] of the whole body focused primarily on the pelvis. The hips are thrust forward or gyrated in a rolling motion and the buttocks clamped together. The toes or feet may be pointed. Some experts advise women to tense their buttocks or point their toes to increase their chances of having an orgasm. Rather like suggesting someone should yawn to induce sleep, this confuses cause and effect. Subconscious reflexes that result from orgasm cannot be applied to cause orgasm.

Regardless of gender we all start out much the same in the womb. A process (called atrophy) inhibits the development of the superfluous anatomy. In the male, the Wolffian ducts develop into the vas deferens (and other tubes required for ejaculation of semen) that connects the testes to the penis. But they waste away in the female. The Müllerian ducts persist in the female to become the uterus and vagina but they disappear in the male.

The male and female external genitalia look identical until seven weeks. The sex (XY & XX) chromosomes determine whether the gonads become the testes (male) or the ovaries (female). The labioscrotal folds become the scrotum (male) and the labia (female). Thereafter the testes and ovaries produce hormones that drive further differentiation (concluded at puberty).

The genital tubercle develops into the phallus, which is the first rudiment of the penis or clitoris. In the male the pelvic portion of the cloaca undergoes significantly more development to become the much larger penis. The difference is that most women never realise they even have a clitoris.

When I masturbate, I adopt a comforting position of lying on my front with the fingers of both hands placed on my vulva. My index fingers massage over the hood of my clitoris and my second fingers over the sides of my labia. While I generate some arousal (by focusing on fantasy) I gyrate my hips gently. But as I get close to orgasm, I rhythmically thrust my hips forward by clenching my buttocks. I then press down more firmly into the spongy tissue either side of the labia (immediately below the pubic bone). The clitoral organ is pressured between my fingers and pelvic muscles.

As a mature woman (especially if the arousal phase extends for more than a few minutes) vaginal lubrication can get in the way of my fingers providing the stimulation (traction of dry fingers) that I need to orgasm. Also the area alongside my labia remains swollen after orgasm. Gently stroking over the glans is mildly pleasurable and there is a tiny blip of sensitivity.

3.2.1 Only some women think they orgasm through intercourse

When we talk about consensual sex who exactly is consenting and what are they consenting to? Women may consent to intercourse but consent is a long way off sexual pleasure and no proof that a woman has an orgasm.

Heterosexual lovemaking, for the most part, relies on a man stimulating a woman. Genital stimulation (both manual and oral) tends to rely on the man offering to stimulate the woman and asking the woman to stimulate him. Women don't tend to ask nor will they always allow a lover to stimulate their genitalia, which is no evidence of pleasure let alone orgasm.

Porn portrays women apparently having orgasms with a lover through intercourse, oral sex and masturbation. But Shere Hite found that a majority of women said these techniques were not reliable ways to reach orgasm. Over two thirds (70%) said intercourse was NOT a regular source of orgasms. Over half said they could not reliably orgasm though oral sex (58%) or by masturbating with (or by being masturbated by) a lover (56%).

Sex experts recommend orgasm techniques to women as if they are infallible. No one remarks on the different anatomy but also the very different stimulation provided by each of these approaches. So male masturbation involves massaging the sheath of skin covering the shaft of the penis up and down over the glans. Likewise intercourse and fellatio provide similar stimulation with the addition of a wet and warm environment. In contrast a woman's masturbation techniques involve massaging the internal clitoral organ with pressure from her fingers and pelvic muscles. A vibrator throbs and buzzes. During intercourse a penis thrusts into her vagina (an organ with zero sensitivity) as the man's groin squashes the labia and clitoral bud. Cunnilingus gently stimulates the glans of the clitoral organ in a warm and wet environment. Yet the clitoris is not intended to penetrate a vagina.

I have had thousands of orgasms through masturbation alone and a few tens of lesser climaxes with a lover (never through intercourse[21]). I do not see how anyone can orgasm as a receiver of intercourse. In the first place, no one can orgasm with zero sensation. But also there is nothing remotely erotic about a mating act from a female perspective (being impregnated).

Secondly it is unreasonable to attempt orgasm using stimulation you cannot control. You need to ensure that stimulation continues up until orgasm. It is also preferable that stimulation then ceases. Intercourse is determined by a man's responses so it is unlikely that a woman could orgasm through intercourse even if the vagina was sensitive to stimulation (which it is not).

3.2.2 The G-spot explains the orgasms women think they have

Inexperienced women explore various parts of their body before discovering orgasm but most women (84%) masturbate by stimulating the clitoris. Yet some women today will still buy G-spot wands and phallic vibrators.[22]

There are some sex experts who refer to clitoral stimulation as if it can be directly substituted for vaginal stimulation. They imply that intercourse can stimulate the internal clitoral organ through the walls of the vagina.

Frankly this does not happen. Even when a woman has a clitoral erection, the general pubic area is engorged but the vagina itself is largely unaffected. There may be some slight increase in sensitivity during intercourse but not nearly enough to cause orgasm. Much like the G-spot theory, the clitoris has been used to justify so-called vaginal orgasms. It is a shame that ignorance and political conviction that vaginal orgasms must be possible distort our understanding of women's sexual anatomy and what is realistically achievable by any woman (who is not trying to please men).

Men engage in intimate relationships because of their need for penetrative activity with a lover (that is sometimes combined with a desire for affection). Men cannot accept that intercourse appeals to them because they are male. They think that all we have to do is wave some magic wand and overnight women will want intercourse as much as they do. This explains why the G-spot is promoted so universally despite its total ineffectiveness.

The Swiss researcher Andrea Burri talked to over 3,000 women. The study (the biggest of its kind to date) concluded that the G-spot as a well-defined area did not exist. The findings appeared in the Journal of Sexual Medicine (2010) yet they have had little impact compared with the success of the original theory. Burri was shocked that such a small sample of women had been used as the basis for promoting this small area at the front of the vagina (never proven to be erectile tissue) as the means to enable every woman in the population to orgasm from the stimulation of intercourse.

It's easy to identify an area of the vagina and give it a name. It is much more difficult to prove that such an area is capable of producing an orgasm. The G-spot is simply an explanation for the orgasms some women think they have. Consequently it only works one way. This explains why it is utterly futile for a woman to use information about the G-spot to have an orgasm. It is easy enough to establish that the vagina is inert but mere scientific fact will never stop women suggesting that vaginal orgasms exist.

3.2.3 Relatively few women ever use a vibrator to masturbate

Sex toys are a useful addition to a couple's sex play: to take the pressure off a man having an erection and to provide stimulation that does not necessarily lead to orgasm. But many gimmicks bought in embarrassment and ignorance are never used. Lying on her back exposes the vulva and can be a good position for a woman to offer intercourse. But orgasm is achieved by the combined stimulation of fingers, pelvic muscles and body weight on the clitoral organ. A woman uses a thrusting motion to masturbate that involves lying on her front. This is incompatible with using a vibrator.

Companies sell vibrators to women so we naturally assume that they must succeed in using them to masturbate to orgasm. These fashion trends are driven by our love for hi-tech accessories backed by marketing campaigns. A vibrator is a piece of hard plastic. Unlike the real flesh and blood penis, there is nothing inherently erotic about a gadget. I am aroused by my lover and by focusing on his erection, his mind and his ability to ejaculate.

Men do not use vibrators to masturbate because they know that physical stimulation is instinctive and relatively trivial, once a person is mentally aroused. A vibrator provides a tingly sensation but (unlike when using fingers) it cannot massage the tumescent erectile tissue of the clitoral organ by pressing either side of the labia. There is nothing wrong with women enjoying pleasant vibrations but stimulation alone does not cause orgasm.

Basic concepts like feeling comfortable with your own nudity and being familiar with your own genitals are fundamental to enjoying sexual activity of any kind. [23] But only women ever attend masturbation clinics, which try to increase women's self-esteem by providing knowledge about sexual anatomy (their own rather than a man's). A man doesn't tend to need help with these issues because he enjoys observing and stimulating his penis.

Only mammals employ a thrusting technique to mate, which extends the male's pleasure (not the female's). Some women claim that a sex toy is more effective than a penis in stimulating them to orgasm. But women can't evolve an ability to orgasm that depends on the invention of a gadget hundreds of thousands of years after the emergence of our species.

If the vagina had evolved the ability to respond to an external stimulus (which would make it the only internal organ of the body to be touch sensitive in this way) then it is much more likely to respond to the stimulation provided by a penis than by a sex toy. This proposed orgasm technique, aimed only at women, has literally been invented by the sex toy industry!

3.3 Understanding what works: erotic versus emotional stimuli

If men were attracted to responsive women, presumably they would hope for a woman who could orgasm within say 5 seconds of being stimulated. In reality, a man needs a woman to offer intercourse for as long as he takes to ejaculate (no more no less). But a woman has no control whatsoever over how long the stimulation she obtains from intercourse will last for.

Some women show off by talking about sex (naturally they mean intercourse) as if they need it as much as a man does. It's as if a woman orgasms every time a man offers her an erection but at no other time.[24] Try asking women what turns them on and they haven't a clue! Women typically suggest an assortment of possibilities, most of which are not remotely erotic. It is clear that women expect only emotional sensations from intercourse.

Sexual arousal starts as a subconscious response to eroticism in the brain. We become conscious of arousal because this trigger increases the flow of blood into the pelvic area. In turn this increased blood flow causes the genitals to become more sensitive to stimulation. For men this increase in sensitivity is very significant. But a woman is typically unaware of arousal.

In men the increase in blood flow causes a significant stiffening of the genital structures (particularly the penis). In younger women there is little discernible swelling of the genital structures but in older women (over the age of forty) there can be some noticeable swelling around the labia indicating tumescence (but not rigidity as in the male) of the clitoral organ. This increase in sensitivity of the penis or clitoris when combined with a mental focus on eroticism (either the innate eroticism of the sexual activity or imagined scenarios) enables a person to stimulate themselves to orgasm.

Muscular tensions in the pelvic region increase, culminating in a peak that is suddenly dissipated (providing a sense of release). Orgasm involves the sporadic contractions of the muscles, sensations of ejaculation of semen (men only as there is no equivalent female sensation) and the sensation of the extra blood (accumulated in the genitals) flowing away from the area.

Young women are unaware of clitoral tumescence. Nevertheless the sensations of arousal and orgasm are identical to older women who experience this physical phenomenon. So women masturbate to orgasm with similar frequencies throughout their lives until menopause. But their responsiveness with a lover only develops in middle age (if at all). The main benefit of clitoral tumescence is an increased sensitivity in the pelvic area during sexual activity with a lover, who provides the correct internal stimulation.

24

3.3.1 Female arousal is more deeply buried in the subconscious

Sexual phenomena (such as masturbation or gay sex) tend to be shocking and alien until we discover we enjoy them. Similarly once we experience arousal, we see the positive (rather than the offensive) aspects of eroticism. Anyone who objects to eroticism does not understand the nature of arousal.

There is a belief that we all need sex.[25] But women experience neither sex drive nor the associated sexual frustration. Men are aroused by sexual thoughts or discussions. Once a man is aroused, he can suffer significant frustration if intercourse is not available. This explains why many writers of erotic fiction are women. Female arousal is like a deep pool within a woman's subconscious that she may be able to dip into from time to time.

As a mature woman, stimulation of the clitoral glans together with vaginal fisting or anal intercourse (causing tumescence of the internal anatomy) leads reliably to climax. In a similar way to masturbation, first of all I have to decide whether my mind has the ability to respond to erotic scenarios.

During sex, I need time for my mind to tune into the sensations of being stimulated. During masturbation I have to spend a considerable time coming up with a fantasy that gets my mind going. Sometimes I have to give up! I have only around twenty fantasy scenarios (mostly derived from erotic fiction) that I have used for orgasm over the years. Of these I use only 4 or 5 on any regular basis. The one I have used the most often came from male homosexual erotic fiction that I read when I was still a teenager.

Before contemplating orgasm (alone or with a lover) I need to feel some genital sensation in response to thinking about an erotic scenario. I feel a sense of excitement, perhaps an increase in heart-rate or breathing. When I stimulate my clitoris, I can feel a slight tingling sensation. Mentally I am able to find aspects of sexual scenarios inherently erotic and appealing. If I am not in the mood then the idea of sexual activity does nothing for me and eroticism that would normally arouse me can seem quite unexciting.

A woman has to push her way towards orgasm at every stage with studied concentration. At no point is orgasm inevitable except once it is already happening. I cannot see how female orgasm is possible while sleeping because it is such hard work even when fully awake. But also the psychological environment of dreams is not intensely focused enough to lead to orgasm. I seldom have sex dreams but, if I do, they are romantic scenarios based on the prospect of vaginal intercourse. Strangely I never dream either about my masturbation fantasies or about my own sexual relationship.

3.3.2 Women's arousal depends on a more indirect mechanism

Men are turned on as a direct consequence of their drive to penetrate (a female) and thrust until ejaculation. A woman lacks this drive. Women are not naturally aroused by either sexual activity or genitalia[26] as men are. A woman aged 29 said she couldn't understand why a 70-year-old man would still want to chase women. She said *"surely by that age enough is enough!"* Women rarely appreciate the strength of some men's sex drive.

The fact that BDSM can be used for arousal is a reflection of our fascination with the idea of control (of doing something to someone else). For a woman to respond positively to eroticism, she must identify with the penetrating male's perspective. A woman's fantasies are surreal because female arousal (that causes orgasm) relies on an indirect mechanism of imagining the consequences of men's sex drive to penetrate another person.

Women are turned on more by words than images. Books involve using your imagination but also they provide insights into people's minds: *"As she bent over he caught a glimpse of ... and he imagined what it would be like to be ...."* Images do not have the same psychological significance. One issue may be control. A man typically has control in sexual scenarios and of his own stimulation through intercourse. The mechanism of using fantasy seems to give a woman the opportunity to control the plot and manipulate the participants to create the turn-ons she needs to reach orgasm.

My fantasies focus on abstract concepts of thinking about a man's desire to penetrate and of his penis thrusting until ejaculation. My fantasies always involve fictional men. As soon as I imagine a man I know in real life, the realities of how I see him as a social (rather than erotic) being take over. Intercourse in the context of a relationship has never been erotic enough to work as a fantasy. There is no taboo, suspense or sexual tension. Thinking about fellatio is a turn-on because the activity is highly explicit.

Once my mind tunes into an explicit fantasy I can orgasm within less than a minute or two. My fantasies develop in stages. There is the initial buildup or scene-setting where I determine whether my mind is responding to the anticipation of sexual excitement. Then I home in on the aspects of sex that I know from past experience are most likely to arouse me sufficiently.

Once I feel the tension start to build, my mental focus (which blocks out all awareness of my physical surroundings) is on the fantasy until I reach orgasm. It's difficult to say where the sensations of orgasm come from. The process is much less predictable with a lover when I don't use fantasy.

3.3.3 Women are aroused by fantasy, not real-world turn-ons

Men are aroused by thinking about sexual activity with someone they find attractive. Only two thirds (69%) of women ever have erotic fantasies. The rest (31%) admit that they have never once been aroused by thinking about eroticism. They are not even aroused by thinking about their own partners. But this makes sense because women's fantasies typically involve fictional men rather than real men.[27] Given their fantasies do not reflect real life, women are unlikely to find arousal and orgasm easy with a real-life lover.

Personally I need to focus on male genitals, male sexual psychology (a man's focus on his erection and his urgent need for penetration) and the male satisfaction in ejaculating. His eyes and kindly words just don't do it for me. These attributes may be romantic but they do not help with orgasm.

We need to differentiate between general turn-ons and the mental focus on explicit aspects of eroticism that enable us to reach orgasm. For example, women's breasts may cause male arousal but not male orgasm. Otherwise a woman could just show a man her breasts instead of offering intercourse.

Breasts are associated solely with females so they are naturally of interest especially where there are variations between different females. If the only time a man sees a woman's breasts is when he has sex, then breasts also become associated with sexual opportunities. This fascination with the size, texture and look of a part of the body is something quite unknown to a woman. Women do not have the same fascination with male anatomy.

From a fantasy perspective, a woman can imagine engaging in surreal sexual activity with complete strangers. But in real life a woman does not have a sex drive so she is not aroused by the idea of doing something sexual to someone else but rather the idea of something sexual being done to her. This is a consequence of women's passivity in real-life sociable scenarios.

A woman's ability to get aroused relies on her appreciation of a man's sex drive and the idea that a man is aroused. This less direct arousal mechanism relies on the higher brain function of connecting cause with effect.

Women are slower to arouse with a lover because the more subconscious focus of receiving stimulation (clitoral and penetrative) from a lover is much more subtle (indirect) than the mechanism of using conscious fantasy. The more subtle turn-on of enjoying the idea of penetration by a lover during sexual activity only becomes effective once a woman is mature enough (over the age of thirty-five) to be responsive with a lover (if she also has clitoral erections as she ages this may help facilitate arousal).

IV   Sexual techniques and exploring sex play with a lover

Men do not make ideal lovers of women. Not only do they orgasm easily but men rarely appreciate what drives women emotionally or how women stimulate themselves to orgasm.[28] We assume that only older generations viewed sex as a forbidden and taboo subject. But where are all the liberated couples today willing to discuss the sex play, they use to bring variety to their sex life? Few couples ever invest in communication or sexual knowledge to improve their lovemaking. Most people view sex as a personal and emotional experience rather a chance to learn sexual techniques.

The tiny minority, who has an active interest in sex, often assumes that everyone is sexually insatiable as if we all think about sex in the same way. But we don't. Nor should we in a healthy and balanced society. Some people are much more sexually active and responsive than others. In a competitive world, more is always equated with better. Yet there is no evidence that the highly-sexed are any happier than those who have low sex drives.

There is no such thing as normal. Neither is it ideal for us to have an average sex drive any more than there is a disadvantage in having a low or a high drive. We are naturally satisfied according to our sexual appetite.

In the early years of a relationship, hopefully passion leaves little room for discussion! And for many couples, sex remains an implicit part of their relationship they never discuss. Other couples find it helpful, over time, to take a more explicit approach to sexual pleasuring. Heterosexuals tend to default to intercourse-to-male-orgasm so, inevitably, exploring other sexual techniques involves effort, trust and an investment in communication.

Nearly all the orgasms I have ever had, regardless of whether I am alone or with a lover, involve lying on my front with my eyes closed. While masturbating my intense focus on fantasy provides a sense of sexual release quite different to climax with a lover, which takes longer. With a lover I need to focus on the sensations of being penetrated (anal intercourse combined with clitoral stimulation). Fisting stimulates the vestibule of the vagina and may provide a woman with a unique kind of climax. I masturbate by moving my hips rhythmically but with a lover I lie relatively still.

It is, of course, the height of pretension to recommend sexual techniques to complete strangers. If a woman hopes to benefit from my conclusions, she will need to identify with my experiences including discovering her own arousal through fantasies and her own orgasm through masturbation. Couples need a strong relationship to discuss sexual preferences openly.

4.1 Proposing and planning sex sessions, providing sex talk

When a man has a new lover the novelty makes sex more exciting for a while but gradually he falls back to having intercourse with similar frequencies as before. Couples have intercourse more frequently when young but frequencies decrease over time.[29] Research indicates that this decrease in activity is due to aging rather than to tiring of sex with the same lover.

We assume that people become less sexually active as they age in the same way that they become physically less active. This is not so. Only men's responsiveness reduces with age. Female responsiveness (which is always lower than men's) changes little as women age. So couples have intercourse less frequently over time because of the decline in male sex drive.

Some women say they stop having orgasms. But you cannot forget how to orgasm! Women's sexual behaviours involve making conscious effort (to varying degrees) to provide a (simulated erotic) response to intercourse. This explains why women lose interest in intercourse over time but their true responsiveness through masturbation does not reduce as they age.

By providing turn-ons women make money, have fun, satisfy their vanity and find a mate! But men are confused when women appear to want sex but don't. Even with a positive attitude towards eroticism, a woman is much less driven by sexual opportunities because of her lower responsiveness. A woman's amenability depends on her willingness to please a lover.

It's important to differentiate between a woman's possible states of mind. She may be totally switched off. In which case forget it! She may be up for a quickie. In which case go for it! Or she may be willing to engage in a longer sex session based on, occasional mutual pleasuring, but more typically being pleasured by a lover. Be grateful and make the most of it!

Planning sex sessions ahead a little helps get the female brain in the mood for sexual pleasuring. Start a sex session with a relaxing bath followed by a massage for the woman. I like my lover to admire my body and talk about what he would like to do to me. My fantasies focus on a man wanting to penetrate me. Women's fantasises often revolve around men's sex drive.

Tell her what you are thinking as you stimulate her from behind! I advise talking in terms of urges, domination and possession rather than the graphic visual detail that men enjoy. I like my lover to stroke the area between my legs (from clitoris through to anus). I like him to hold my butt cheeks apart both before and as he penetrates me. I want him to use a hand to hold me firmly down as he dominates me (only with my permission!).

4.1.1 Regularity of intercourse relies on male responsiveness

One would expect the regularity of intercourse to depend partly upon a woman's motivation. But Kinsey found the rates of sexual outlet (made up mostly of intercourse) for married men who are early adolescents to be about twice as high as the outlet of men who become adolescent later. This was the same difference he found for single men (whose outlet is primarily masturbation)! So intercourse frequencies correlate with male sex drive.[30]

This is hardly surprising given intercourse has nothing to do with female orgasm. Some women openly admit their schemes to avoid sex, for example, by going to bed at different times. They succeed because their partners are too timid to insist. Such tactics do not work with a highly-sexed man.

Men may complain about a lack of sex in marriage but not every man is willing to leave his wife and possibly his family to get it. Men with low sex drives may be able to put up with a sexless marriage later in life. But men with a high drive cannot imagine life without sex. So the system is self-regulating to a degree because such men simply find another woman.

An Indian woman explained that she stopped offering intercourse once they had more children than they could feed. But her husband just went to prostitutes instead. She concluded *"Men must have a vagina!"* She decided to risk more children so that her husband's income would support her family (rather than prostitutes). As populations grow, our survival will depend on our ability to face emotional rather than technical challenges.

Men are true innocents! They claim to have no idea of the deception their fantasies force on women. The idea that a woman enjoys sex (or is assumed to have an orgasm) validates men. The fact that she may have to be cajoled into bed does not strike men as a contradiction. The emotional bonding process makes this behaviour core to men's sexuality. A man's pleasure is assumed. But as women rarely initiate or drive sexual activity, a man seeks some reassurance that a woman is sufficiently enthusiastic about intercourse that she will continue providing a regular sexual outlet.

Men in turn are bemused and confused by women's contradictory behaviours. There is so much talk of women enjoying sex and wanting sex as much as men do. Many men then find that their wives and girlfriends are rarely that keen. Men are left trying to guess when might be a suitable time to suggest sex. There are no sources of advice. Even asking the question is embarrassing because it reveals a possible failing on someone's part given the universal promotion of intercourse as a natural instinct for everyone.

4.1.2 A woman may offer intercourse when she feels respected

After fifty years of marriage one woman told me she had never been interested in men. Men tend to seek women out. Women don't need intercourse. They get affectionate companionship from their girlfriends and their children. Men often overlook the wider relationship after decades together.[31]

There are many more men (than women) looking for casual sex. Consequently, men cannot have sex as easily as women can. So men look at porn in the absence of the real thing. But why would a woman ever need porn? If they want to get laid, most women can easily find a very willing partner!

The most common form of prostitution services straight men and the second most common services gay men (only 4% of the male population!). Prostitution is least common among gay women but even straight women pay male escorts for companionship rather than sex. Men pay for sex because (regardless of a relationship) sex provides them with a sense of emotional intimacy. Unfortunately, it is not possible to buy the loving intimacy (based on respect and affection) women hope for when they love someone.

If a woman holds back on offering sex, a man (hopefully!) feels that something worthwhile has been won when he gets it! A man is empowered by having made a sexual conquest and in public he may be tempted to flaunt his success as ego. Penetrative sex reflects well on a man (who takes his pleasure) but not on a woman (who offers to pleasure her lover). Anyone who offers their body to a man does so because they hope not only that their lover will be grateful but also that he will respect them for the offer.

No wonder men have trouble understanding women! Men's idea of bliss involves penetrating a vagina and thrusting for two minutes until ejaculation. Men's gratitude, including their willingness to pay a woman's way, indicates their implicit acceptance that they obtain a pleasure from sex that is not entirely reciprocated. Yet ego prevents men from admitting that sex involves women doing them any favours, which seems a little ungenerous!

Some men have an emotional need to justify the pleasure they obtain from a woman's body especially in the context of a loving relationship. A man assumes a role of pleasuring a woman in order to differentiate himself from other men. He looks for personal validation as a lover. He wants a woman to acknowledge his ability to deliver pleasure through intercourse (primarily). This is what makes sex political. Naturally, some women respond to this political and sexual pressure. Either some adults are incredibly unworldly or they are in denial of the facts they don't wish to acknowledge.

4.1.3 Married men have sex more often than single men do

Despite the complaints, research indicates that married men have more sex[32] than single men do. Men may look for other pleasures when they pay for sex but they are usually happy to settle for intercourse with their wives. So men may fantasise about (apparently available) single women but, ultimately, they return home to have sex with their girlfriends and wives.

Kinsey concluded that men determine intercourse frequencies. Men find this difficult to believe because they feel controlled by female consent. In truth, it is a compromise between male sex drive and a woman's willingness to indulge her lover. Some men push more than others, especially if they don't use masturbation. I was constantly aware of my partner's frustration. My own responsiveness would involve offering perhaps monthly (but for a few consecutive days). But I offer weekly frequencies to avoid my partner becoming moody. This once-a-week pattern becomes a chore.

A married man has ways of getting sex. He suggests that a woman's lack of sexual interest proves that she does not love him. He complains that his balls ache if he does not ejaculate regularly. Sperm are invisible to the naked eye so even millions of them do not add up to more than a fraction of a man's ejaculate. The prostate gland (at the base of the penis) contributes most of the fluid in the semen. The discomfort is due to the tiring of the muscles involved in maintaining an erection. There is no lasting harm.

In the past women were indebted to men for their protection and their children's. Today if a woman expects a man to hang around and put up with all the emotional trauma of a relationship then she has to incentivise him. It seems likely that relationships are more likely to last (survive the hurdles that tend to arise over the longer-term) if they are founded in love (a stronger emotional connection) because of the inherent generosity that is involved when one person loves another (as opposed to a relationship based purely on the enjoyment of physical attributes and sexual activities).

In theory, a woman could easily offer intercourse to any half-decent man. But most women avoid casual sex, not just to avoid pregnancy and disease, but also because of the universal and huge taboo over female promiscuity. Despite male fantasies of arousing women to orgasm through intercourse, they evidently don't accept that women might have a sex drive as men do.

Men assume they have the right to look elsewhere as if intercourse has no emotional significance for them. But intercourse is vital to a man and he expects a woman to behave as if having sex with him is significant to her.

4.2 Showing sexual initiative and providing erotic feedback

Doesn't anyone else find it odd (and very convenient!) that modern advice on female orgasm just so happens to reflect almost exactly how women's responsiveness is portrayed in pornography? Real women are obliged to exaggerate their apparent responsiveness to encourage a lover to keep going and to substitute for the much more obvious signs of male arousal.

Given a woman's much lower responsiveness, she will never orgasm every time a man does. But she can still provide a lover with a simulated erotic response. By making small moans or sighs she can assist with her lover's orgasm as well as provide a form of erotic feedback that indicates when stimulation is pleasurable. Women grease the wheels of sex[33] so to speak!

During intercourse a woman can move in rhythm with the man's thrusting. She can kiss and caress him affectionately. By assisting with penile stimulation a woman contributes towards the goal of intercourse: male orgasm. Intercourse is like an erotic dance where a woman follows her lover's lead.

Men assume that women are aroused (as men are) by talking about sex. I am not totally immune to suggestion but it does not have the direct impact on my desire to have sex as it seems to for men. Women are not aroused by talking about sexual activity in general. Women may flirt by making sexual references thereby indicating their amenability to a man they fancy.

In porn the actors, unlike their female partners, communicate very little. They grunt occasionally and they have an expression of focused concentration. This is to be expected. Anyone who is aiming for orgasm needs to concentrate their mind on the turn-ons and enjoy the stimulation at hand.

So what is the purpose of the facial expressions porn actresses use? They are ways of communicating a sexual come-on or a form of enticement. A woman can use her facial expression or body language (such as mouthing a half-peeled banana!) to emulate sexual activity that appeals to men.

But where do the female vocals come from? My theory is that the biological origins of intercourse come from a mating act that involves a male assault or a male subduing a female. There is an inherent turn-on in the violent objections of someone who is being penetrated against their will.

I use a range of resistance scenarios in my fantasies from a man cajoling the woman to relax (her anus) and accept his erect penis to forcing himself on her regardless. Aspects of control and domination, as well as the idea of a man negotiating his own pleasure, are core to my ability to orgasm.

4.2.1 Women's talk of orgasm does not lead to more sex for men

Ironically (because only male responsiveness declines with age) women are often more sexually active when younger. Once a woman has children, she is much less motivated by sex. Women are more confident about admitting that intercourse does not cause orgasm as they age, by acquiring status or wealth or through education. Women today say they have orgasms with a lover but they are no more amenable than older generations.[34]

Andrea Burri, the Swiss researcher, notes that female sexual dysfunction (FSD) is increasing because we have unrealistic expectations for our sex lives. Most women don't have any expectations and so they never complain. FSD is defined not in absolute terms (of facts or techniques used) but in terms of how upset a woman is by her failure to orgasm with a lover.

Any objective assessment of human sexuality must conclude that while sex may be a frivolous form of entertainment for (at least some) men, it involves a much more serious emotional and relationship commitment for most women. More realistic sex information needs to acknowledge these key differences in our sexual and emotional responses. Women are simply not equipped, physically or emotionally, to respond erotically with a lover.

For men, any lower body contact with an attractive partner is erotic and therefore, to varying degrees, emotionally fulfilling. Men perceive women to be inhibited because they assume that women should naturally be aroused as men are by physical proximity to a lover. In fact women's lack of responsiveness means they do not respond to sexual scenarios as readily as men do. This is not inhibition but simply the way women have evolved.

Both sexes feel responsible for female orgasm through intercourse and the resulting taboo makes it difficult to find answers. Telling women that they should orgasm through intercourse causes disappointment and frustration. Women end up accepting their unresponsiveness as an excuse for not making any effort in sex. Telling women they need to take an interest in sex for their lover's sake (in return for his engagement on more emotional and romantic interaction) may help for those who can cope with such honesty.

Women's genitalia change significantly as they age. I found that increased vaginal secretions made intercourse more comfortable over time. Given I always knew what arousal and orgasm felt like (from before I was a virgin), I have never found intercourse to be remotely rewarding, either emotionally or erotically. I offer vaginal intercourse when I know my own arousal is unlikely or once I have had a climax through clitoral stimulation.

4.2.2 Some men expect women to make sex exciting for them

Films use sound effects to indicate a couple having sex off-screen: a regular banging (of a bed against a wall) and the woman's vocal accompaniment. Such scenes may represent a turn-on for men but it seems to me that men enjoy making female arousal into a tasteless joke. Male fantasies put tremendous pressure on women to conform to men's view of their sexuality. Female orgasm is more often associated with porn than with real life. Men who watch porn (I realise that is any male with access to a computer!) come to expect every woman (even their wives) to provide these turn-ons.

Some men assume that women enjoy all the activity shown in porn.[35]Many women are never exposed to fictional accounts of how women are supposed to be pleasured by a male lover. Even if they are, not all women are equipped with the sexual instincts to respond by providing an erotic performance. Men seem to think that every woman has the skills of a porn star, a prostitute or a mistress. Such a woman needs to be unoffended by men's carnal instincts and able to put on a convincing erotic show. Some women approach sex with romantic illusions. They assume that a man is so aroused by their body that he can sweep them off their feet with his sexual passion. They may not accept the need to offer any more turn-ons.

Women's responses with a lover are driven by social attitudes. For example, in the past women were often expected NOT to respond to intercourse. Men considered it unseemly for a woman to cooperate with intercourse. Perhaps the idea that a woman might be getting something from the activity put pressure on a man to continue intercourse for longer than he could. This is yet more evidence that women's responses with a lover involve conscious behaviours rather than spontaneous sexual responses. No one can suppress a sex drive to obtain sexual gratification over long periods.

We experience intimacy not just through sex but also through inflicting pain. We hurt others (either physically or by what we say) because it feels good. We obtain a form of personal gratification but this is not necessarily sexual. Women can be bullies as much as men but they are not equipped (physically or emotionally) to get sexual gratification from others by force.

The UK Office for National Statistics Crime Survey 2020 found 98% of sexual assaults (including penetration of a vagina, anus or mouth by a penis, object or other body part without consent) are perpetrated by men. Victims include more women (11.0%) than men (0.7%). Women are more likely to be attacked by a partner or ex-partner (45% of cases). Men are more typically (43%) attacked by a stranger compared with women (15%).

4.2.3 Women's need for affection drives regular relationship sex

While women often fail to appreciate the importance men place on eroticism, men seldom appreciate the importance women place on affection.

Sex is so much more rewarding for women when they feel affection for their lover. In the early days, a man is more motivated to show his appreciation for a lover by being affectionate. In assuming (implicitly or explicitly) that sex is on offer, a man is asking for a favour. A woman's affectionate response gives him the confidence to initiate sex. As the affection dies, sex becomes a mechanical exercise for a woman and a man finds it increasingly awkward[36] to suggest sex or to just assume it's on offer. So women's need for affection drives regular sex within loving relationships.

Sex occurs much more easily in the early stages of a relationship because being affectionate with each other provides the most natural lead-in to sex. First a woman offers some affectionate interaction by touching or kissing her lover. Her lover communicates his desire by kissing back with passion, by touching the woman with an increased focus on the erogenous zones and by indicating his own arousal by pressing his groin against her body.

Some people suggest that being relaxed about nudity is uninhibited. But women avoid being nude because it is highly suggestive to men. Women enjoy intercourse in the early days of a romance. When in love, lovemaking is an expression of a man's devotion to a woman and represents a small part of the quality time a couple spends together. Later, sex tends to focus on satisfying male needs without providing the affection women hope for.

A woman may want children and this instinctive desire may help cause her to be willing to provide a man with regular intercourse. A woman does not need (or want) intercourse over decades. But many women would be devastated if they could never be a mother. Women engage in intimate relationships with men because of their need for affection that can sometimes be combined with an enjoyment of sensual lovemaking with a caring lover.

Despite all evidence to the contrary men insist that women must enjoy sex exactly as they do. But women do not obtain the same kind of comfort from sex. So women need time to develop the much deeper emotional attachment that helps them justify offering a man intercourse over decades.

If we all had men's promiscuous instincts there would be no long-term relationships. Someone has to be tied into one person. A woman does this with no sex drive at all! Quite something if you think about it! Women may be passive in a genital sense but they have a strong emotional drive.

4.3 Bringing variety of situation and technique to intercourse

Although intercourse provides little internal sensation, a woman feels some external pressure. When a man thrusts deeply[37] the base of his penis may thump or brush against her vulva (the clitoris and labia) and perineum (towards the anus). She may enjoy the eroticism of being dominated (from the whole-body contact and his weight) and the psychological satisfaction of being penetrated (from knowing that his penis is deep inside her body).

Quickies often involve a standing position. The woman can support herself against an object (a tree, a table or the side of the shower) or lean over at 90 degrees and rest face down. When combined with rear entry, quickies allow the man to focus on the satisfaction of ejaculating into the woman's vagina. If a woman usually moves her hips, it is pleasant occasionally to have the excuse to do absolutely nothing and let the man do all the work!

For men sexual opportunities seem precious. So they approach sex with a sense of urgency and anxiety. A man holds his erect penis between his lover's legs to find the entrance to her vagina. She may assist by spreading her legs, thereby allowing him to penetrate her vagina more easily. The man then thrusts rhythmically into her vagina as the woman kisses or caresses him allowing the time he needs to enjoy thrusting before ejaculating.

If a man used quickies all the time, a woman could easily end up feeling like a receptacle for his semen. A man should bring some variety to the lead-in, pace and rhythm of intercourse. Men can also use passionate deep kissing and some gentle caressing to make intercourse feel more romantic.

Men tend to initiate sex so it can be a turn-on if a woman takes the initiative either by offering to pleasure him or by suggesting what she would like. A couple can use rear entry or the woman can bring her legs up and hug them around her lover's back. If deep vaginal penetration is uncomfortable due to too much pressure on the cervix, a woman can place her hand down between her body and her lover's to prevent penetration being too deep.

Women can also flirt by playing to men's fantasies. So I might say that having sex outdoors is a great turn-on, I don't mean I orgasm from having sex up against a tree. I am being frivolous and exaggeration is part of the fun! After making sure he has a firm grip on the steering wheel, suggest stopping to have sex. Find a convenient tree in a secluded wood. When out walking through some out-of-the-way countryside suggest having sex discretely behind a bush. When you are lying face down nude sunbathing in a private garden, give your lover permission to penetrate you from behind.

4.3.1 Sexual pleasuring techniques a woman may enjoy

There are no female equivalents to the turn-ons that motivate men sexually.[38] Women often prefer intercourse in the dark and they do not enjoy observing their own genitals. The visual impact of her own and a lover's genitalia can even detract from a woman's enjoyment of sexual pleasuring. This is because a woman prefers a romantic view of sexual activity rather than the harsh reality of hairy genitals and less than perfect body shapes. In men's eyes women can seem impossible to please. But women wonder why men do not provide them with the social interaction they hope for.

A woman does not obtain the same automatic emotional fulfilment from sex that men do. She needs sexual pleasuring to be emotionally meaningful. By offering a man intercourse she hopes that he will care about her because she is, not just sexually, but also emotionally significant to him.

Men tell me that their partners orgasm through cunnilingus. They seem to think that if a woman is stimulated genitally, she always orgasms. This is not my experience. I do not necessarily orgasm even if I do receive stimulation in the correct form. My body only responds to the point of orgasm very sporadically: perhaps once every few weeks for as much as 3 or 4 times in one week but not every week. So how can a man give a woman an orgasm when I cannot do this for myself even through masturbation?

If my lover offers oral sex, I accept his desire to please me but eventually I stop him because the sensations are minimal. Likewise manual stimulation of the clitoris can be irritating or uncomfortable. It is only if I am sufficiently aroused that clitoral stimulation assists with achieving orgasm.

The American researcher Nicole Prause explains her conclusion that women mistake orgasm with a lover. As she points out, this is not a problem if they are enjoying the sexual activity. It is only a problem when such women boast about orgasm as if it equates to the erotic responses that men experience. Shere Hite concluded that women more often talk about enjoying the closeness and intimacy of sex, rather than referring to orgasm.

A woman can enjoy sex for many reasons. She may want the emotional reassurance of knowing that her attractiveness (both her body and her behaviour) arouses her partner. Or she may enjoy indulging her fantasies. Sometimes for a change, a woman may enjoy using a blindfold to focus on sensations and use some low-key bondage to heighten the sense of being desired by a partner. Sex toys can be used to tease, bring in some anticipation (of the real thing!) and take the pressure off a man needing an erection.

4.3.2 Sexual pleasuring techniques a man may enjoy

A woman who lies fairly inert during sexual pleasuring, communicates a lack of cooperation and causes a man to feel sexually unappreciated. Both social and sexual interaction rely on the active interest of the participants. In women's eyes men can seem impossible to please. But men wonder why women do not provide them with the sexual interaction they hope for.[39] Men's erotic fantasies involve exploring sex play in which a woman takes an active sexual interest by responding when her lover stimulates her.

A woman can stimulate a man by licking and sucking gently on his nipples. Have your lover enter your vagina from behind (as he supports his weight on his arms) and tell him to keep his hips still. In this position you can gyrate your hips to stimulate his penis. See if you can make him come just by moving your hips! Tightening your pelvic muscles rhythmically helps.

The facts of male sexuality are evident from observing the real world but they are also supported by research findings. Frequencies of sexual activity vary but the vast majority of men (92%) orgasm quickly and easily through masturbation as well as through intercourse (100% with their wives). Research focuses more on attitudes towards sexual pleasuring (such as women's willingness to provide fellatio) rather than on whether men achieve orgasm (which is perhaps assumed given men's responsiveness!).

If your man loses his erection, have him lie on top of you. Feel around his penis and testicles. Once his penis hardens slightly, hold it firmly in your hand and use a gentle pumping action to increase his erection. Once erect, guide his penis into your vagina. Move your hips to help stimulate his penis. If he moves his weight onto his arms, you can keep moving your hips or alternate with tightening your pelvic muscles to give him more sensation. Reach down and feel around the base of his penis and his testicles. Admire his hardness and hold his buttocks firmly to pull him deeper inside.

For a little variety, plan the occasional session in front of the TV. Using porn movies, to supplement sex, adds a little spice for both lovers. A man also enjoys a woman who uses language that is sexually explicit. Exaggerate if necessary as you describe the things you would like him to do to you!

Offer fellatio whenever you can. I like to offer in the bath or at the start of a sex session. Likewise stimulation of the male G-spot works best in the bath. You need to lubricate a finger and probe gently into his anus. Make sure you ask him for directions. This is an excellent lesson in appreciating how difficult it is give and respond to feedback when penetrating a lover.

4.3.3 Techniques for getting the most out of anal intercourse

Few homosexual men orgasm solely from penetration. The penis is always involved. The anus and the entrance (vestibule) to the vagina have some sensitivity. But the internal organs (vagina and rectum) are much less sensitive.[40] So the kind of stimulation that might lead to female physical arousal includes anal intercourse or using the fingers of one hand (fisting) to stimulate the entrance to the vagina. The sensations of penetration provide a mental turn-on as well as some pleasurable sensations but they do not in themselves cause orgasm. The clitoris always needs to be stimulated.

It might seem perverse to get turned on by anal sex but no one can orgasm from zero stimulation. A significant advantage of anal intercourse (with adequate lubrication) is the increased sensation for the receiving partner. Anal intercourse is also more of a psychological turn-on because it emphasises the woman's vulnerability in offering penetrative sex. A man has to use much more care and consideration. It is not just a banging session.

I am not promoting anal sex. I am simply pointing out that anal sex is the main activity that has ever provided me with any kind of climax with a lover. This fact is provided for anyone who is interested – take or leave it!

Anal intercourse can be pleasurable especially when varied, in rhythm and depth of penetration. But it is vital to know when to give up! It also helps to limit anal intercourse to those occasions when a more mature woman is physically aroused. Patience and time to invest in relaxation and lubrication will also help. Use your body weight to provide a sense of domination.

Although gay men evidently enjoy pleasure from receiving anal sex, heterosexual women are often not interested in the same form of sexual pleasuring. Anal sex is different for a man because of the pleasure from stimulating the prostate and because of his erection. A man should change his rhythm of thrusting by alternating between teasing the glans of his penis in her anus and longer thrusts providing pressure and deeper penetration.

As well as lubrication, also allow some lead-in time to allow for relaxation. Use your hands to spread her arse cheeks and use your fingers to supplement the sensations of penetration. Take her hand and have her feel your erection as you thrust into her. The knowledge that deep penetration has been achieved can be a turn-on in itself. The most comfortable position is from behind with the man on top. Otherwise man on top with woman facing. This position allows for deep kissing. A woman can use her tongue to simulate thrusting in her lover's mouth synchronised with his own rhythm.

V   Sexology should present research not popular beliefs

Why is sexual pleasure taboo? Probably because of the associated exploitation (of women by men) and deceit (perpetrated by women on men).[41] Few people appear to be capable of appreciating objective sex information.

The taboo involved in talking about sex means that most people prefer to say nothing. Political correctness prevents sexologists from questioning and challenging in the way that scientists are obliged to. There is always someone somewhere who is offended! The woman-on-the-street is never invited to comment on (let alone provide convincing evidence in support of) modern theories in sexology. Women are more or less told (often by men) how they should enjoy sexual pleasure. Sexology promotes the same fantasies about female sexuality that every man-on-the-street dreams of!

In every chapter of human history we have shown ourselves to be slow to accept scientific conclusions that conflict with our personal intuition, with our self-interest and with our desire to set ourselves apart from animals.

For example, we know that we are spinning through space on a massive sphere but it is easy to see why our forebears assumed that the earth was flat. In the first instance we trust our intuition and instincts rather than accept the abstract and intellectual logic involved in scientific reasoning.

Wilberforce only succeeded with his 'Slave Trade Act' (of 1807) because of a legal technicality. The moral outrage of slavery was indisputable but slavery had become an essential part of commercial life. Most of us can ignore our moral conscience when it conflicts with our own self-interest.

When Darwin published 'The Origin of Species' (in 1859) he encountered bitter opposition from the Christian Church. Society considered it degrading to compare (and find similarities between) animals and humans. Although we kill and reproduce, we like to see ourselves as spiritual beings rather than acknowledge any of our primitive carnal instincts. We like to think that we are influenced foremost by intellectual and rational thought.

We rarely acknowledge the emotional and political forces that influence the acceptance of scientific work. The truth is that some research findings are much more actively promoted than others with little regard for their merits. We have all heard of Viagra, not because of its efficacy but, because it is backed by the economic might of the pharmaceutical industry. We have also heard of the G-spot because it helps therapists promote intercourse as a core lovemaking act. It is not that more realistic sex information is necessarily ignored so much as that it is simply drowned out.

41

References

[1] The history of science is part of the history of the freedom to observe, to reflect, to experiment, to record, and to bear witness. (Alan Gregg)

[2] There are boys who never masturbate. There are boys who masturbate twice or thrice in a lifetime; and there are boys and older youths who masturbate two and three times a day, averaging 20 or more per week throughout periods of some years. (Alfred Kinsey)

[3] ... it is difficult to understand what mechanisms could produce ejaculation without a precedent orgasm. The confusion in the literature seems to be the result of making the term orgasm and orgastic pleasure synonymous. ... there are admittedly occasions when there is little pleasure accompanying an ejaculation. (Alfred Kinsey)

[4] Originally the pre-adolescent boy erects indiscriminately to ... emotional situations ... sexual or non-sexual .... By his late teens the male ... rarely responds to anything except a direct physical stimulation of genitalia, or to psychic situations that are specifically sexual. (Alfred Kinsey)

[5] In a short-term prison, the majority of the men ... may go for long periods of months, or for a year or more, without ejaculation. ... most of them live comfortably enough, apparently because there is little erotic arousal which needs to be relieved by orgasm. (Alfred Kinsey)

[6] The highest incidences of the homosexual, however, are in the group which most often verbalizes its disapproval of such activity. (Alfred Kinsey)

[7] In the sexual history of the male, there is no other single factor which affects frequency of outlet as much as age. (Alfred Kinsey)

[8] The boys who are earliest adolescent, by age twelve at the latest, are the ones who most often have the highest rates of outlet in the later years of their lives. (Alfred Kinsey)

[9] The very fact that upper level males fail to get what they want in socio-sexual relations would provide a psychologic explanation of their high degree of erotic responsiveness to stimuli which fall short of actual coitus. The fact that the lower level male comes nearer having as much coitus as he wants would make him less susceptible to any stimulus except actual coitus. (Alfred Kinsey)

[10] It would be difficult to find another situation in which an individual who was quick and intense in his responses was labeled anything but superior. (Alfred Kinsey)

[11] The gifts that are bestowed by males of all social levels upon girls with whom they keep company many be cloaked with fine sentiments, but they are, to a considerable degree, payment for the intercourse that is expected. (Alfred Kinsey)

[12] The upper level male dislikes the limitation on petting in his relations with prostitutes. He commonly complains about the genital inadequacies of the prostitute, ... that she is not responding erotically. In consequence, she does not stimulate the emotionally sensitive, upper level male. (Alfred Kinsey)

[13] My husband doesn't seem to enjoy anything besides intercourse, and that very briefly, and I don't know what to do to change him. I've tried hard. (Shere Hite)

[14] It is a mistake to assume that a sophistication of techniques would be equally significant to all persons. For most of the population, the satisfaction to be secured in orgasm is the goal of the sexual act,

and the more quickly that satisfaction is attained, the more effective the performance is judged to be. (Alfred Kinsey)

[15]Most of the action in a petting relationship originates with the male. Most of it is designed to stimulate the female. (Alfred Kinsey)

[16]Differences in how women and men experience orgasms can lead to unrealistic expectations and a misinterpretation of the meaning of sexual response. (Tatnai Burnett)

[17]Since most males are aroused by seeing female breasts, and because most females are, in actuality, only moderately aroused by having their breasts tactilely stimulated, female breasts may be more important sources of erotic stimulation to males than they are to females. (Alfred Kinsey)

[18]There is great pressure on women in our society now to say they like 'sex'. (Shere Hite)

[19]Although the male is frequently aroused without completing his response, he rarely engages in such activities as masturbation or coitus without proceeding to the point of orgasm. On the other hand, a consideration portion of the female's sexual activity does not result in orgasm. (Alfred Kinsey)

[20]One of the most striking aspects of a sexual performance is the development Of neuromuscular tensions throughout the body … There may be occasional moments when the movements cease and the muscles are held in continuous tension; but … there is usually a flow of continuous muscular movement from the first moment of arousal to the moment of orgasm. (Alfred Kinsey)

[21]I never fake orgasm. I am angry with other women who do, because then men can tell me that I am incapable sexually, because I do not have vaginal climaxes, and other women they have slept with do. Since I have never had a vaginal climax, I question their existence. (Shere Hite)

[22] … there are exceedingly few females who masturbate by inserting objects into the vagina, and most of them who do so are novices, exhibitionistic prostitutes, or women who have had such procedures recommended to them by male clinicians. (Alfred Kinsey)

[23]More than three-fourths (81 per cent) who had never masturbated recognized that they had not done so because they had not felt any need for such an outlet. (Alfred Kinsey)

[24]Nearly all (but not all) younger males are aroused to the point of erection many times per week, and many of them may respond to the point of erection several times per day. Many females may go for days and weeks and months without ever being stimulated unless they have actual physical contact with a sexual partner. (Alfred Kinsey)

[25] … the basic value of sex and intercourse for women is closeness and affection. (Shere Hite)

[26]Females… are much less often attracted by observing the male partner, his genitalia, or other objects associated with the sexual performance. (Alfred Kinsey)

[27]The sexual partners in these dreams were usually obscure and unidentifiable – an epitomization of some general type of person; and even the actor in the dream was not always the dreamer, but a person who combined the capacities of an observer and a participant in the activity. (Alfred Kinsey)

[28]Many males, however, basing their concepts on their understanding of coitus and upon their conceit as to the importance of the male genitalia in coitus, imagine that all female masturbation must involve an insertion of fingers or of some other object into the depths of the vagina. (Alfred Kinsey)

[29]Males who are married between 16 and 20 start with (intercourse) frequencies which average 3.9 (times per week) for the population as a whole… Frequencies drop steadily from the teens to about 2.9 at age 30, 1.8 at age 50, and to 0.9 at age 60. (Alfred Kinsey)

[30] ... the married males who have the highest total outlets, most of which depend upon high frequencies of marital intercourse, are for every social level, those who become adolescent first. ... this indicates that the wife's part in determining the frequency of marital intercourse is not as important as one might expect (Alfred Kinsey)

[31] Considering the physical advantage which the married individual has in securing intercourse without going outside of his own home, it is apparent that the older single male develops skill in making social approaches and finding places for sexual contact which far exceed the skills of married persons. (Alfred Kinsey)

[32] The mean frequencies of total sexual outlet for the married males are always, at all age levels, higher than the total outlets for single males... (Alfred Kinsey)

[33] Mutual responses in a socio-sexual relationship are also significant because the one partner may respond sympathetically to the reactions of the other partner. The male may become emotionally aroused when he observes that his wife is aroused, and he is particularly liable to be aroused when he is in physical contact with her and can feel her responding. (Alfred Kinsey)

[34] this improvement in the quality of the coitus ... had occurred coincidently with some reduction in the frequencies ... It is our impression that today the males of the younger generation more often limit their contacts to the frequencies which their wives desire. (Alfred Kinsey)

[35] The average college-bred male is more likely to extend the pre-coital petting for a matter of five to fifteen minutes or more. (Alfred Kinsey)

[36] The male's difficulties in his sexual relations after marriage include a lack of facility, of ease, or of suavity in establishing a rapport in a sexual situation. (Alfred Kinsey)

[37] Psychologic satisfaction in knowing ... sexual union and deep penetration have been effected. ... Tactile simulation coming from the full body contact ... and from his weight. (Alfred Kinsey)

[38] ... promiscuity may depend, in many instances, upon the male's anticipation of variation in the genital anatomy of the partner, in the techniques which may be used during the contacts, and in the physical responses of the new partner. None of these factors have such significance for the average female. (Alfred Kinsey)

[39] When she fails to be interested in sexual relations with her husband, when she is less interested than he is, when she refuses to have intercourse as frequently as he would like it, when she refuses to allow the variety in pre-coital techniques that the male would like to have, or when she accedes to such techniques without evidencing an interest equal to that of the male, she is encouraging him to find extra-marital relations. (Alfred Kinsey)

[40] The anus, like the entrance to the vagina, is richly supplied with nerves, but the rectum, like the depths of the vagina, is ... poorly supplied with sensory nerves. However, the receiving partner ... often reports that the deep penetration of the rectum may bring satisfaction (Alfred Kinsey)

[41] As long as sex is dealt with in the current confusion of ignorance and sophistication, denial and indulgence, suppression and stimulation, punishment and exploitation, secrecy and display, it will be associated with a duplicity and indecency that lead neither to intellectual honesty nor human dignity. (Alan Gregg)

www.ingramcontent.com/pod-product-compliance
Lightning Source LLC
Chambersburg PA
CBHW060526280326
41933CB00014B/3106